frogs in the aquarium

SO-AXY-408

by werner von filek

Originally published in German by Franckh'sche Verlagshandlung, W. Keller & Co., Stuttgart/1967 under the title *FROSCHE IM AQUARIUM*. First edition © 1967 by Franckh'sche Verlagshandlung.

Distributed in the U.S.A. by T.F.H. Publications, Inc., 211 West Sylvania Avenue, P.O. Box 27, Neptune City, N.J. 07753; in England by T.F.H. (Gt. Britain) Ltd., 13 Nutley Lane, Reigate, Surrey; in Canada by Clarke, Irwin & Company, Clarwin House, 791 St. Clair Avenue West, Toronto 10, Ontario; in Southeast Asia by Y. W. Ong, 9 Lorong 36 Geylang, Singapore 14; in Australia and the south Pacific by Pet Imports Pty. Ltd., P.O. Box 149, Brookvale 2100, N.S.W., Australia.
Published by T.F.H. Publications, Inc. Ltd., The British Crown Colony of Hong Kong.

Contents

Unorthodox thoughts instead of a foreword 5

1. "FISH" WITH FOUR LEGS 7
2. FISH AQUARIA—FROG AQUARIA 13
   Plants . . . Tank size
3. A QUICK LOOK AT SOMETHING ELSE 17
   Bombina . . . The terrarium . . . Food . . . Spawning
4. WHO'S WHO IN THE PIPID WORLD 25
   The South American species: Identification . . .
     Aquaria . . . Activity
   The African species: Keeping *Xenopus* . . . Identi-
     fying *Xenopus* species . . . Identifying *Hymenochi-*
     rus . . . Keeping *Hymenochirus*
5. PROBLEMS WITH THE FROG MENU? 50
   Xenopus . . . *Hymenochirus* . . . *Pipa*
6. CHARACTERISTIC FEEDING BEHAVIOR
   OF PIPIDS 62
   Pipa . . . *Hymenochirus* . . . *Xenopus*
7. PIPIDS DO NOT BELIEVE IN THE STORK 67
   Rain . . . Artificial inducement . . . *Pipa* reproduc-
     tion . . . Spawning *Hymenochirus* . . . *Xenopus*
     reproduction . . . The Hogben test . . . Spawning
   Just a few words about the skin
8. THE CURIOUS TADPOLES OF THE GENUS
   HYMENOCHIRUS 87
   H. curtipes . . . *H. boettgeri*
9. TADPOLES WITH ANTENNAE 93
   Xenopus tadpoles . . . Feeding . . . Growth

Frontispiece: An adult *Xenopus laevis.* Notice the lidless, bulging eyes and the large mouth. The webless fingers help separate frogs of the genus *Xenopus* from the smaller *Hymenochirus* species. Photo by G. J. M. Timmerman.

Unorthodox thoughts instead of a foreword

Many thousands of words make a book, and when the author has at last got his collected thoughts together, put into words, he has to produce a foreword as well. He has to put words in front of words. Is that not asking too much? To put his picture in front would be more appropriate, but since it would then be a fore-picture—no, this is too obviously self-praise! Thus the author asked for a foreword is in a fix. So he sits down at his desk and writes out the contents, a sort of preview of what makes up the essence of the book. In just a few sentences, the most striking parts of his work have soon been condensed. And, rather pleased, the at first so undecided author forwards his "foreword" to the publisher. The latter adds a few numbers, puts the vocable "Table of Contents" above it, and reminds the tarrying author of the foreword, long overdue. That is the position I find myself in just now.

You, however, my dear readers, want to get to know frogs. You have bought the book to gain insight into the biology of batrachians, very specific, particularly interesting batrachians, and not to be confronted with the problems of an author. Please do not be annoyed with me—for the following pages will lead you away into the kingdom of aquatic frogs. And if I can arouse in you just a fraction of the enthusiasm that I myself feel for my beloved anura, then you will make me happy, very happy in fact. Then we will see each other again, perhaps in front of an aquarium with frogs.

Werner v. Filek

The Metric System

This book uses the metric system, which is a more international method of measurement than the English system of inches and feet. One meter (m) is equal to 1000 millimeters (mm). A centimeter (cm) contains 10 millimeters and is 1/100 of a meter. One inch is equal to about 2.5 cm or 25 mm. Roughly, 4 inches are about equal to 100 mm; 6 inches = 150 mm; 1 foot = 305 mm; 3 feet = 914 mm. The number of millimeters divided by 10 gives the number of centimeters.

As to liquid measures, the liter (l) is commonly used. One liter is slightly less than one U.S. quart. A liter contains 1000 milliliters (ml). The unit cubic centimeter (cc) is approximately the same as one ml.

To convert degrees Centigrade to degrees Fahrenheit, multiply degrees Centigrade by 1.8, and then add 32.

Good base temperatures to remember: 0°C = 32°F; 10°C = 50°F; 20°C = 68°F; 30°C = 86°F; 100°C = 212°F.

1
"Fish" with four legs

"The desire to keep a fish in a bird-cage," Edgar Genet once said, "characterizes the surrealist." But vivarists are not surrealists, they are realists, and realists keep fish exclusively in aquaria. Aquaria are, therefore, the environment of fish brought into the dwelling place of humans. That's how it is as a rule, but it is not, as we shall see, *the* rule.

What does the aquarist find so fascinating about his aquaria? I have taken the trouble to question about a dozen *Tubifex* buyers in a pet shop, and have asked every one of them the above question. But if you think that they all gave the same answer, you are mistaken. I took home about a dozen different opinions: "Every day the brilliant colors of the fish fill me with new enthusiasm," one of them said; the next one is "fascinated by the insight into another, strange world." The third one finds it calming to watch the barbs, and yet another aquarist is animated by the hope of cultivating a particularly rare species. Most, and at the same time least of all, was said by the last one questioned: "The fish are my hobby."

In spite of these very different opinions, they all agreed on one aspect: they had all spoken about fish. All of them, without exception, kept fish in their aquaria. That aquaria are, or should be, inhabited by fish is a preconceived idea. I declare war to this idea and, as inhabitants of the aquarium, I recommend "fish" with four legs! My hobby is frogs, and yet what I have at home are not terraria but mere aquaria. It stimulates and relaxes me to watch my frogs, and I am as fascinated as the *Tubifex* buyers when I look into the strange underwater world of my aquaria. But in my aquaria there are no fish, just frogs,

7

nothing but frogs. At first my tanks, too, were inhabited by colorful, interesting fish, but the frogs have taken away my sympathy for them—or, more correctly, they have "swum away" this sympathy.

Now he is already confusing aquaria and terraria, some of you will say, and particularly resolute characters will probably even make tapping gestures with the index finger against the forehead. Forgive me—I owe you an explanation. Hence the misunderstanding!

Frogs are usually kept in terraria. That is correct, if we think of tree frogs, not just our green tree frogs (*Hyla*) but the extraordinarily colorful tropical varieties, or the plump warty toads.

Although tree frogs (family Hylidae) are not popular pets in the United States, they are fairly popular in Europe and the Orient. The larger species, such as this golden tree frog *(Hyla aurea)* from Australia, are long-lived and easy-to-care-for pets. Although *Hyla* requires moisture, very few species are aquatic.
Photo by G. Marcuse.

Toads are common in most parts of the world and are greatly respected as insect eaters. Their dry, often spiny skin is an adaptation to habitats which have little free water. Many species are burrowers, and some even thrive in deserts. *Bufo viridis* (above) is an attractive European species. Southern South America is the home of *Bufo arenarum* (below). Photos by Van Raam (above) and G. Marcuse (below).

Most frogs begin their lives as tadpoles with fringy external gills, a ventral mouth, and no sign of limbs. Of course, every rule has its exception, so there are frogs hatched without gills, some with well-formed limbs, and even a few with dorsal mouths. Some of the pipids belong to this latter category. Photo by H. Pfletschinger.

That is the rule, but this rule, too, is confirmed only by the exceptions. And the exceptions consist above all of "fully aquatic" frogs.

What, now, does "fully aquatic" mean?

The development of frogs, as we all know, is a perfect example of the transition from the aquatic to the terrestrial life of vertebrates. The larval stage usually begins in the water, whereas the mature frogs inhabit damp homes on land. The changes of their respiratory organs run parallel with this development, and from gills to lungs we find all the different forms in the frog kingdom, not forgetting skin respiration, of course. Naturally there are some outsiders among the 2,500 frog species in existence today, not just anatomically or those whose behavior shows quite specific peculiarities, but also a few who do not, or not quite, go through the standard process of development characteristic for anura (= tailless amphibians; often called "salientia" as well). To these belong, for instance, those species which continue to live in the water when they are adult frogs. They are the fully aquatic or purely aquatic frogs.

In the other category we find the predominantly aquatic species, those living in the immediate vicinity of the water, as well as the terrestrial forms. Predominantly aquatic frogs take refuge in the water if there is danger, they are excellent swimmers and divers, but they always go back to the shore. Furthermore, they hunt and feed exclusively on land. Typical examples are the fire-bellied toads and numerous *Rana* species such as the edible frog (*Rana esculenta*) and the leopard frog (*Rana pipiens*).

Fully aquatic frogs, on the other hand, constitute only a small group and their members belong to widely differing families. Thus we know of purely aquatic species from the family of "true toads" (Bufonidae), the family of discoidal-tongued frogs (Discoglossidae), as well as from the families of Leptodactylidae and Ranidae. Some of these species have quite adventurous names, such as *Ooeidozyga laevis*.

With regard to some species, there is reason to believe they only secondarily returned to a purely aquatic way of life. Fully

There are probably no frogs which are afraid of the water, but there are many species which are dependent on water for food and protection. *Rana clamitans*, the common green frog of the northern United States (in the southern states it is brown and is called the bronze frog), is often found on the shores of lakes and ponds. When frightened, it seeks safety underwater by burying itself in the mud or silt at the bottom. Photo by M. F. Roberts.

This South American bullfrog (*Leptodactylus pentadactylus*) is a moderately aquatic member of the very large frog family Leptodactylidae. The species of this family vary in size from one-half inch to over nine inches; some build nests on land and lay eggs which develop directly into gill-less miniature versions of the parent. At the other extreme are the fully aquatic species such as *Calyptocephalus gayi* (now commonly called *Caudiverbera caudiverbera*). Photo by G. Marcuse.

aquatic frogs often exhibit certain common peculiarities which are partly explained by the adaptation to an aquatic life: the tendency to have broader, flattened heads, wider jaws, long slender fingers, etc.

Among the purely aquatic frogs there is one completely related group—the family Pipidae. All pipids—and they include about 15 species distributed over four genera—always, without exception, live in the water. It is to these that this book is dedicated above all, not only because they are an ideal example of fully aquatic frogs, but also because the pet shops keep offering these species. Pipids are not difficult and delicate, they are by no means demanding, and yet one can experience a host of interesting adventures with them in the field of natural science.

2
Fish aquaria — frog aquaria

The term "fish aquarium" almost sounds like "old geriatric" and similar linguistic blunders. But we merely want to emphasize the difference from "frog aquaria". Are not both quite similar, is there not water in both of them? Certainly, but a few differences do exist and we shall briefly deal with these. The first question we have to clear up at the very beginning is whether the frog keeper-to-be prefers optically attractive tanks, that is tanks with plants, beautifully decorated display aquaria, or whether he is more practical minded and quite content with purely functional aquaria. Equally important is question number two; that is, what species (singular or plural) the vivarist is going to choose or has already chosen. Everything depends on the answer to these two questions, not least the satisfaction of the keeper and the suitability of the advice I am about to give.

Plants

The naturalist with aesthetic demands on his aquaria is advised to specialize in the genus *Hymenochirus* (one of the four pipidean genera). These clawed frogs are only a few centimeters long, make good-natured movements and leave the plant stock alone. They climb about adroitly among the *Vallisneria* leaves and thus offer additional entertainment. But part of the aquarium must remain free from plants. For, if the aquatic plants grow too densely, we cannot observe the animals properly. And it is that, after all, which every vivarist wants to do.

Where pipidean frogs are concerned, plants to increase the oxygen content are not required, as all species dealt with here breathe through lungs which they regularly fill up with fresh air at the water surface. This breathing sometimes takes place very

Hymenochirus species are active little frogs which like to climb about in dense vegetation. This type of setting is easily produced by grouping several good sprigs of *Myriophyllum* or a similar plant in one corner of the tank. A *Myriophyllum* jungle like this one should provide hours of entertainment for the enthusiastic frog-watcher. Be sure that most of the tank is barren, however.
Photo by C. D. Sculthorpe.

temperamentally. The use of a glass plate is, therefore, advisable, or, conversely, the aquarium is not filled to the rim. For the larger species of the genera *Xenopus* and *Pipa,* the aquarium must be covered at all times. Apart from that, all rules and hints' referring to a fish aquarium also apply to the *Hymeno-chirus* tanks.

Xenopus as well as *Pipa* species are coarse fellows, and their unmannerly behavior is usually fatal for delicate aquatic plants. *Xenopus* occasionally rakes up the ground and if the latter consists of fine river sand you can imagine the effect this has on the flora and the clearness of the water. It is best, therefore, to choose coarse material for the bottom layer of *Xenopus* tanks.

If you insist that plants decorate the frog aquarium, you are advised to put flower pots into the aquarium or to bury them in the bottom material. By placing a grate on the bottom you offer your plants even safer protection from being brutally uprooted. That nothing but hardy plants must be used is self evident after what I have just said. Some species, for example *Xenopus mülleri*, like to float on the water surface. They hope to catch the insects which are playing about above the water surface or dropping onto the water. Such successful hunting can be observed without difficulty. A stock of floating plants seems to be very welcome to these experts. A floating branch has been recommended, but I regard this as superfluous since I have never seen pipids voluntarily leave the water.

Since *Xenopus* seems to enjoy uprooting plants, one is forced to use mainly floating plant species when decorating the aquarium. One of the best choices is the floating form of the water sprite (*Ceratopteris thalictroides*). This beautiful plant does well in warm aquaria and grows rapidly. Photo by Dr. J. Stodola.

Hiding places, however, definitely need to be provided, especially in aquaria with no or a sparse plant stock. The simplest way to go about this is to supply a halved flower pot. When constructing ingenious caves one should avoid tempting the animals to spend their life in hiding; their game of hide-and-seek would vex the vivarist.

Tank size

The size of the tank, finally, depends on the individual species and, of course, on the number of frogs kept. Another crucial factor is whether the vivarist intends to attempt cultivation. Breeding tanks for *Pipa pipa* and *Xenopus,* for instance, should have a minimum capacity of 70 liters (dimensions about 60 x 30 x 40 cm). An exception is once again the *Hymenochirus* species which can be induced to spawn even in very small containers. The size 24 x 24 x 44 cm being suitable for breeding tanks.

A recipe for frog aquaria guaranteeing 100% success, however, exists no more than for fish aquaria; successes cannot be forced and failures cannot be avoided completely. A lot of experience is certainly useful, but it alone is no guarantee either. The greatest luck invariably goes to the careful, attentive keeper, the conscientious one, who furnishes and looks after his containers according to the basic principles of animal care, that is: adequate light, warmth, and cleanliness.

3
A quick look at something else

A quick look at something else shall be permitted; for a short time we will leave the pipids. Let us start with fire-bellied toads. We had best begin with the keeping of one of the two species living in central Europe. The material is easy to obtain, can be added to at any time, and, apart from that, European anurans are easier to care for than the exotic ones. These toads do not, of course, quite fit the scope of this book because the *Bombina*

Although most species of frogs belong to the advanced families Hylidae, Bufonidae, Leptodactylidae, or Ranidae, there are several genera of primitive frogs which have to be placed in other families. The midwife toad (*Alytes obstetricans,* also known as *Obstetricans obstetricans*) is one of the European members of the primitive Old World family Discoglossidae. Photo by W. Lierath.

species are not fully aquatic frogs but are anurans which are predominantly dependent on the water. They belong to the family of the discoglossids ("discoidal tongues"); other members of this family, apart from the toads, include the "Painted Frog" (*Discoglossus pictus*) and the Midwife Toad (*Alytes obstetricans*). Their habitat is the aquaterrarium with a strip of land and a shallow water basin.

Bombina

On the other hand, however, these toads as much as the pipids are primitive frogs, and they have many behavioral characteristics in common, for instance the male in heat seizing the female around the loins. If you cannot, therefore, decide on keeping pipids right away, the following excerpts from the life of toads is dedicated to you. These excerpts are meant as a

Alytes is famous for its habit of carrying the eggs attached to the back. This terrestrial frog mates on land in the normal way, but the egg strings become wrapped around the thighs of the male. Although he occasionally moistens the eggs, the male remains on land while carrying the strings. Just before the eggs hatch, the male finally enters a pond or stream and the eggs hatch into typical tadpoles. *Alytes* has lived up to 20 years in captivity. Photo by W. Lierath.

The family Discoglossidae includes three common genera: *Alytes*, *Bombina*, and *Discoglossus*; other genera occur in Africa and Asia. The painted frog (*Discoglossus pictus*) is an uncommon species in captivity and is shyer than most frogs. Its habits are not as unusual as those of *Alytes*, and its coloration not so spectacular as that of *Bombina*. Photo by G. Marcuse.

guide to the care of toads, always, however, with the ulterior motive of the keeping of "true" aquatic frogs, the pipids, soon to follow.

Undoubtedly every nature-lover has already seen a toad, the lively dark gray to black, warty batrachians with the irresistibly beautiful red- or yellow-speckled belly. They haunt the small muddy waters and their characteristic cries of "oonk-oonk" sound partly sinister and partly mocking. That there are two species in European zones is less well known—to many people, "a toad is a toad". And indeed, up to the end of the 19th century only one species was recognized or known at all, and when one has come to realize the difficulties of differentiation—the differential characteristics are anything but marked—it is not hard to see why. Let us, therefore, begin with the differentiation of the two central European species: the Fire-bellied Toad (*Bombina bombina*) and the Yellow-bellied Toad (*Bombina variegata*). What is most irritating about the toads is that the belly of the Fire-bellied Toad is often of a yellow color and that of the Yellow-bellied Toad quite frequently red. And it is precisely the color that would be such an obvious differential factor. In our toads, however, it varies so much that it cannot be relied on for systematic classification.

A better way to determine the species is to examine the fingers: *Bombina bombina* has tiny, just visible webs between the fingers; in *Bombina variegata* this webbing is completely absent. Then there is the "stroking test." Stroke the skin of the back with the inside of your fingers. If the skin feels rough but not jagged, it is very likely the Fire-bellied Toad, whose warts are covered with small, rounded-off horny swellings. If, on the other hand, one gets the impression of stroking across sharp, scratching thorns, these will be the horny spines of *Bombina bombina.* Another good differential characteristic has been des-

Bombina variegata, the yellow-bellied toad, almost always has a yellow ventral surface. The fingers are devoid of webbing, and all the digits are dark. Although the skin is rough to the touch, there are no spines present to produce the scratchy effect noticed with *Bombina bombina.*

Bombina bombina, the fire-bellied toad, usually has a red belly, although yellow is also commonly found. The fingers have small webs near their bases, and the thumb and inner toe are colored the same as the belly. Also, the fire-bellied toad has spiny tips on the warts, causing a scratchy effect when rubbed with the finger.

cribed by Birken-Meyer (1948): if the same bright red or yellow color can be seen on the inside of the first fingers or the underside of the first toes, it is *Bombina bombina*; if, however, the toes are dark, gray-black, we have *Bombina variegata* in front of us. The males have an additional distinguishing mark. The *Bombina bombina* males have internal vocal sacs; on their throats, even when they are resting, we can observe a bulge which is not present in the males of *Bombina variegata*.

The terrarium

For the toads we acquired or caught ourselves and whose species we have identified, we now need to furnish a suitable home. A medium-sized aquarium with a flat stone island rising up from out of the water (if possible not in the center of the tank) will do nicely. The island can be covered with moss pads or all sorts of marsh plants. Hiding places should also be provided. The water level in this aquaterrarium is best adapted to the natural living conditions of the animals, and should be a maximum of 20 cm. Aquatic plants—especially in breeding tanks—are recommended.

Put the toads into the container and, after a short period, one will be horrified to find that the animals keep moving restlessly along the glass walls and time and time again try to climb up the glass. Do not worry! After one or two days the toads become completely acclimatized to their new surroundings and their restlessness will disappear. They will then spend most of the day in the water, lying on the surface in the sunshine or waiting for possible prey near the shore. At night they often leave the water but remain in the immediate vicinity of their favorite element (even if the size of the aquaterrarium permits longer excursions). Just in case, the toad tanks should be covered with a grate, or perhaps with a glass plate, because occasionally even the toads feel the call of the open air, and once a toad has got out of the container it dies of dehydration within a very short period—much more quickly than other anurans which also require moisture.

Food

As far as toad food is concerned, the little chaps fall to with enthusiasm when given earthworms (also mealworms in some cases), flies, smooth caterpillars, and small butterflies. Grasshoppers are very popular tidbits as well. Once a wasp or a bee gets into the tank it, too, will become a victim of toad greed. It is important, however, that the prey moves. Only then will it be noticed (by sight) and accepted.

Spawning

Both toad species spawn in early summer (April to June), as far as there is a definable spawning season at all. It should not be difficult to put the animals into a not too small aquaterrarium, furnished true to nature, for reproduction. A detailed description of their breeding behavior would be beyond the scope of this book. I shall, therefore, confine myself to just a few points which I will list briefly.

As already mentioned, the female is embraced round the loins by the male; the clasping reflex is released by the movement of the partner. The spawn is shed several times at short intervals, but always in the water. The several hundred eggs are attached to plants. Release from the embrace occurs after a characteristic signal of the female: the legs are stiffly stretched backwards and the body vibrated slightly. Including their gelati-

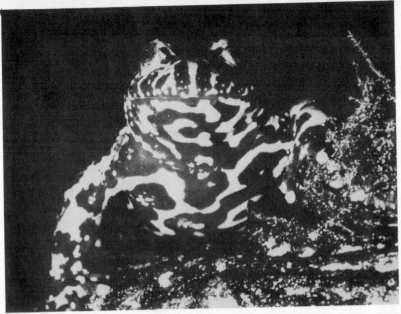

Of the several Asian species of fire-bellied toads, the most commonly seen is probably *Bombina orientalis*, from eastern China and adjacent areas. In this species the bright ventral color is complemented by a bright green and black back, as contrasted to the dark brown or black back of the European species. The bombinas are rather long-lived animals, some having been kept for almost 10 years. Photos by W. Mudrack.

nous coverings, the eggs have a diameter of about 5 mm. Development, from the depositing of the egg to the metamorphosed frog, takes about four to six weeks, depending on the temperature and nutrition offered.

After this brief report on the life of toads we shall now deal with one special characteristic of these animals: the so-called "boat position." Strong stimuli, especially if the animals are handled roughly when taken out of the water, bring about an akinetic condition in them, a kind of rigor. The toad bends its back concavely and both the front and hind limbs are turned outwards, and pressed against the back. The colorfully marked belly is then clearly visible. The animals remain in this position for a long period. A quite similar phenomenon can be observed in the pipidean genus *Hymenochirus*. Although no reference to this exists in the literature, I regularly succeeded in provoking this "boat position" in *Hymenochirus boettgeri*.

As interesting as the lively toads may be, as rich in variation as is the observation of their behavior, they in no way come up to the pipidean frogs. Whereas toad life takes place mostly on the water surface and in shallow areas off the shore, the pipids rule the depth of the water. There they hunt and feed, rarely rising to the surface—and then usually only to get air. To house pipids in an aquaterrarium would mean not being able to watch their fascinating behavior. But we want to keep frogs which are able to compete with exotic fishes. We not only want to look at the water but into the miniature pond; we want to enter the kingdom and life of the pipids. May I begin with the introduction?

4
Who's who in the pipid world

Even when discussing permanently wet aquatic frogs, the driest subject is systematics. But we simply cannot leave out this chapter.

Where do the pipids stand in the famly tree of batrachians? To give a definite answer to this question would mean to know more than the scientists. For the system most frequently applied, that devised by Noble in 1922, is today opposed by a second one which is based on the morphology (science of external and internal structural relationships of animals) of tadpoles: Orton's system (1957). The position of pipids in the anuran system involves a choice between two differing opinions. On the one hand, as a family closely related to the family of "discoidal tongued frogs" (Discoglossidae), they may belong to the suborder Opisthocoela (so called owing to the presence of convex-concave vertebrae); or, on the other, the pipids, together with some Mexican burrowing frogs, form a suborder of their own along with three other suborders. Which of the two systems is the most valid is of little importance to the practitioner in zoology, the vivarist.

Characters

The important point is that both systems recognize the pipids as a complete, separate group having a number of important characteristics in common. The tongue is absent in all pipids; they are, therefore, also called "tongueless" (Aglossa) at times, as opposed to frogs possessing a tongue (Phaneroglossa). They owe their popular name "clawed frogs"

As a general rule, the frogs of the family Pipidae have some or all of the following characters: 1) no tongue; 2) no eyelids; 3) toes with horny claws; 4) fleshy tabs along the sides of the body. There are, of course, exceptions. Some species of *Pipa* lack claws, *Pseudhymenochirus* has eyelids, and *Hymenochirus* has the fleshy tabs very small and indistinct. Thus *Xenopus* is the only genus which has all of the characters of the family. Photo by G. Marcuse of *Xenopus sp.*, probably *X. laevis.*

to the horny claws on three (or two) inner toes, but these claws are not present in all species. Furthermore, the pipids have no eye-lids (sole exception: *Pseudhymenochirus*) and, finally, they are characterized by possessing side or lateral organs, particularly easy to detect in *Xenopus.* These are numerous small, cone-like epidermal structures, arranged as if to form a pattern, and distributed on the head and sides of the animals. Apart from that, the little pipid tribe is connected by a common ecological factor, and that is their purely aquatic way of life. With regard to behavior, too, there are marked parallels, as we shall see later on.

The tadpoles of pipids also have common characteristics; they possess pairs of spiracles, while the other batrachians have only one respiratory opening which is asymmetrically placed. All in all, there is an obvious relationship between the peculiarities mentioned and the way of life. The characteristics of pipids, which we also use as a rough guide for the differentiation of species, are mostly specific adaptations to the permanent aquatic life.

In a manner of speaking, the recent pipids (those still existing today) inhabit two "islands". The genus *Pipa* lives in South America and the other genera on the African mainland. Most pipids inhabit the tropical zone and are found in the waters of the tropical forests. Only a few species are found regularly in water bodies in plains or mountain areas. When discussing the individual species I shall say more about this. Today we know a total of 16 or 17 species and subspecies of pipidean frogs belonging to four genera: *Pipa, Xenopus, Hymenochirus,* and *Pseudhymenochirus.*

THE SOUTH AMERICAN SPECIES

The South American genus *Pipa* has been known longest. In the year 1705, Sibille von Merian described these curious "toads", or rather only the "Alveolar Toad" (*Pipa americana = Pipa pipa*) from Surinam, and for a very long time this one species remained the only one known. Not until the beginning of the 20th Century were the other *Pipa* species found and described. Today five species are know to scientists: *Pipa pipa, Pipa parva, Pipa snethlageae, Pipa aspera,* and *Pipa carvalhoi.* In all these species the female carries the eggs in pouches on its back. The pipas can be identified immediately by their fingers, which are the origin of the old name "star-finger toads": each finger ends in a star-shaped organ, a formation of four rays presumably functioning as a receptor of touch.

Looking at the shape of all five *Pipa* species, one immediately notices that this group divides into two. On the one hand, flat broad forms—the term "cow pat" would be excellently suited to describe these shapes—and, on the other, smaller, less flattened species which to some extent remind one of the African clawed frog *Xenopus*. The two large species are *Pipa pipa* and *Pipa snethlageae*.

Unfortunately, most of these species seldom or rarely reach the pet shops, and with a bit of luck the vivarist may at best be able to obtain *Pipa pipa*. But going to a bit of trouble to get a few pipas definitely pays off, as we shall see later on.

Pipa is not the only frog which carries its eggs in special pouches in the skin of the back. The unrelated *Gastrotheca marsupiata*, a South American tree frog, also has the same habit. *Gastrotheca* is an attractively patterned frog with habits very much like those of some species of *Hyla*, except for its unusual egg-carrying habit. Although its toe disks are small, it is a good climber. Photo by G. Marcuse.

Pipa pipa is the only species of the genus normally found in the pet trade, and when it is available it commands a good price. These bizarre frogs are said to be common in northern South America, but their shape, color, and fleshy head tabs prevent them from being recognized as living animals when they are accidentally collected with bottom mud and debris. These same traits probably also let the frogs' prey come within range before the fish or insect realizes that it is in danger. Photo by H. Schultz.

Also, there is a hope that in the near future the import situation will improve. We shall, therefore, briefly discuss the rare *Pipa* species as well. For this much is certain: they have enough peculiarities.

Identification

If a pipa is offered to the vivarist and neither the supplier nor the dealer are able to give further information about the animal, the following procedure may help to identify the species. First take a look at the hind legs. One has already heard the name "clawed frog", so, of course, the obvious thing to do is to have a closer look at the claws. But here we already get our first surprise: only one *Pipa* species—*Pipa carvalhoi*—has three claws; *Pipa aspera* and *Pipa parva* have two, and in the well-known *Pipa pipa,* as well as in *Pipa snethlageae,* they are absent. Let us remain with the latter two. If these two species are to be differentiated by their external appearance, one best begins by inspecting their finger tips; the star-shaped organ of *Pipa pipa* consists of four rays which in turn have four spikes at the end. These spikes are absent in *Pipa snethlageae.* Over and above this, *Pipa snethlageae* possesses numerous tentacle-like processes in the mouth and esophagal region, whereas in *Pipa pipa* we find, in addition, large skin flaps—flat appendages with frayed ends—in the corners of the mouth and one at the tip of the jaw. This should do us for the time being.

But now we still have to differentiate *Pipa parva* and *Pipa aspera,* the two-clawed species. Here the only guide for the vivarist is the star-shaped organs, which are of a strange shape in *Pipa parva*: two rays of the "stars" are long and the two remaining ones are markedly shorter. In *Pipa parva* we can also observe a weak onset of webbing between the fingers.

The large flat species are distinguished from the rounder dwarf pipas by yet another peculiarity: in the small species the eggs sink into the dorsal skin of the female and the individual pouches close up, but the alveoli of the large species remain open and can be recognized at first sight. The size of the eggs differs: *Pipa carvalhoi* and *Pipa parva* have very small eggs (maximum size 2 mm) whereas the other three species produce large eggs. Another characteristic phenomenon runs parallel with the size of the eggs: pipas with small eggs hatch tadpoles from the pouches of the mother, but the forms with large eggs leave the alveoli as complete little frogs. With regard to alveolar toads, one can, therefore, speak of a direct development.

Information on the habitat of *Pipa* species is scanty. The species *Pipa carvalhoi,* not described until 1937, was collected in Brazilian waters about 1000 m high; after a heavy rainfall the toad could even be found onshore. *Pipa parva,* occurring in Colombia and Venezuela, also was found on the shore. But these observations are not evidence for an incompletely aquatic way of life of the pipas. *Pipa aspera* is known from Guyana,

Pipa snethlageae only from the delta of the River Amazon, and *Pipa pipa* from many parts of northern South America.

In many scientific works and reference books the names *Hemipipa* and *Protopipa* appear along with *Pipa*, i.e., three genera are mentioned. The grouping of the five species described into three genera was made by earlier authors and based on the teeth of these animals. Even in Noble's classical work on the biology of amphibians, there is still the division into *Protopipa* and *Pipa*. The genera were finally unified by Dunn (1948), a herpetologist to whom we owe the most extensive description of all South American pipids.

Aquaria

The keeping of pipas involves little difficulty. Just one requirement is an absolute necessity: a large aquarium. *Pipa pipa*, the largest of the pipids, especially demands a lot of space. The average size of this species (length from head to vent) is 120 mm (Dunn even reports as much as 200 mm). As a comparison, *Pipa parva* is only 40 mm long. Rabb bred *Pipa pipa* in a 70-liter aquarium, but I would say this size has to be regarded as a minimum. At the University of Vienna (Institute of Zoology), breeding succeeded in a tank with a capacity of roughly 280 liters—a large aquarium, certainly, but considering the reproductive behavior alone it can by no means be called too large.

Activity

During the day the animals lie inertly on the ground, usually in a dark corner of the aquarium. Often they crowd together and often come to lie one on top of the other. In the twilight they are slightly more active, but all in all are by no means very lively. When coming up for air, however, or when the pipas have been startled, they—and one really would not expect this of them—turn out to be extremely lively, agile swimmers. That these frogs can also react as fast as lightning is shown when they feed, and when they mate their agility increases considerably. The water temperature in the *Pipa* tank should not be lower than 20° C, and becomes ideal at 26° C. A large plant stock is not very favorable as the pipas have obvious difficulty in catching the food animals among the thick growth of the plants. Conversely, the plants suffer under the vigorous swimming strokes or when the animals search for a hiding place. A few, more decorative, large plants are probably best. The water level can be chosen by the vivarist as he wishes; Rabb, for instance, found a water depth of a mere 28 cm sufficient in his aquaria, whereas the animals I observed appeared content at a water level of about 80 cm.

THE AFRICAN SPECIES

Keeping *Xenopus*

One of the attractions of a circus undoubtedly is the clown. If you like such attractions in the aquarium, keep *Xenopus*. Not any particular species, just *Xenopus*; all representatives of this genus resemble one another, not only in their appearance but in their tomfoolery. Quite in contrast to the often portly pipas, *Xenopus* species are lively fellows, always active, always hungry, and—so it appears to the observer—always filled with a sheer insatiable curiosity. *Xenopus laevis* is the best-known species and also the one most frequently offered on the market. Not only zoologists and vivarists are interested in *Xenopus laevis* but also gynecologists and medical laboratories. For *Xenopus laevis* is also used as a test animal in the diagnosis of pregnancy (more about that later). Accordingly, reports on the keeping and care of *Xenopus laevis* are numerous and there is no shortage of good, but unfortunately often contradictory, advice. The following basic rules, however, should be adhered to by every vivarist, as they apply to all *Xenopus* species.

First the favorite temperature: an average temperature of 26 - 28° C can be recommended. One has to bear in mind that *Xenopus* species are particularly tough when it comes to tolerating both lower and extremely high temperatures. Dickinson (1949), for example, reports that *Xenopus laevis* can survive values between 40 and 50° C without being any the worse for it, whereas Lerch (1948) records a low temperature survival record of 2 - 3° C. According to many scientists, the animals should be kept cooler in the winter. Those who want to cultivate *Xenopus* should not ignore this advice! The animals have a

Fire-bellied toad, *Bombina orientalis. Discoglossidae.* Photos: W. Mudrack.

resting period and with the rising thermometer also show a rising vivacity. Although every author recommends an ideal water level, so to speak, the depth of the artificial pond is quite immaterial. But with the *Xenopus* tank also, provisions should be made to prevent the animals from leaping out of the container. Aquaria for *Xenopus* species are equipped with coarse sand or, better still, gravel for the bottom layer, as this will stop the water from becoming turbid due to overly temperamental movements. Likewise, the plant stock has to be adapted to the lively activity of the frogs; here, too, large water plants should be chosen.

As opposed to all other pipids, the differentiation of the two sexes is very simple in *Xenopus* species. The females are easy to identify. They have three lobular appendages at the opening

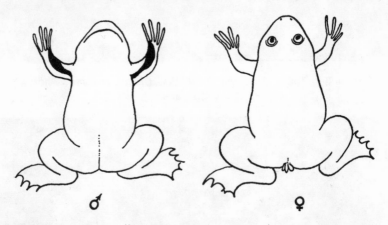

Although the other pipids can usually be sexed only by general body build, the female being stouter than the male, *Xenopus* is often easy to sex by more certain methods. Although the dark stripes of rough tissue on the underside of the forelegs of the male develop only when he is ready to mate, they are easily recognizable when present. The cloacal lobes of the female are often very small and difficult to see, but any specimen with distinct lobes is certainly a female.

of the cloaca. These appendages can be seen from above. *Xenopus* males can be recognized in the mating season or when in mating condition by the dark stripes, then particularly notice-

This female *Xenopus laevis* has well developed cloacal lobes. The fleshy tabs on the sides of the body are also very distinct. Photo by G. J. M. Timmerman.

able, on the inside of the front legs; these can also be felt, as rough areas, when we stroke them with the inside of our fingers.

Identifying *Xenopus* species

The determination of the species is by no means as simple in the genus *Xenopus* as it is in *Pipa*. Six species are known to date, but to the would-be pipid-keeper they all look very much alike. The top-side of the animals—all species—is of an inconspicuous brown to olive color; their skin is slippery (note that "laevis" means smooth); another characteristic they all have in common is three horny claws on the inner toes. All representatives of this genus have extensive webbing between the toes

Xenopus laevis, large clawed frog. Pipidae. Photo: Dr. Herbert R. Axelrod.

Pipa pipa, Surinam toad. Pipidae. Photo: H. Schultz.

European toad, *Bufo bufo*. Bufonidae. Photo: H. Hansen, Aquarium Berlin.

but none between the fingers; their nostrils are directed upwards. A *Xenopus* is thus easy to identify. But which *Xenopus* species we have in front of us still remains unresolved. As the next step in our systematic investigation, take a look at the eye region. If, just below the eyes, there is an obvious subocular tentacle, a so-called "eye antenna" (which is no more than a continuation of the lachrymal or tear duct), and this reaches about the length of half the eye diameter, then it cannot be *Xenopus gilli* and probably not *Xenopus clivii* or *Xenopus laevis*. In *Xenopus gilli* the eye tentacle is absent, and in *Xenopus clivii* and *Xenopus laevis* it is barely noticeable.

If we, however, continuing with our rough systematics, exclude the species without tentacles and those with very small tentacles, we are left with only three species: *Xenopus tropicalis,*

Perhaps the reason pipids are so popular is not because of their unusual biology and habits but simply because they are so strange in every respect. This head-on view of *Xenopus laevis* not only illustrates the bulging, lidless eyes, but also shows how absurd and un-froglike are these most unusual frogs. Photo by Dr. Herbert R. Axelrod.

Xenopus fraseri, and *Xenopus mülleri.* For these three species, first examine the metatarsals of the foot. *Xenopus tropicalis* and *Xenopus fraseri* possess a horny metatarsal tubercle or metatarsal spur. If the horny element is absent from the metatarsals the frog concerned is *Xenopus mülleri.*

This species is widely distributed and occurs in Zambia, Mozambique, Angola, the Congo, some parts of Nigeria, and in Dahomey. The natives call *Xenopus mülleri* "Hamuru" or "Kisisulu". The frogs are said to have been found in riverbeds, deep springs, and in bathing ponds laid out by the natives. *Xenopus mülleri* grows to a length of up to 90 mm and its back shows a brown-olive to dirty-gray color. On its top-side several black or darkish spots can be seen. The belly is of a lighter, yellowish-white color, and the pupils are encircled by a narrow ring of a shiny golden color. *Xenopus mülleri* was first described by Peters in the year 1844—under the name, however, of *Dactylethra mülleri.*

The next species we shall look at is *Xenopus tropicalis.* This species is dark olive on the back, yellow-white on the belly, and the throat is often marked with delicate brown specks; it occurs in stagnant as well as in fast running waters of forest areas in Guinea, French Africa, and even as far as Angola. The eyes of *Xenopus tropicalis* are relatively small.

And now *Xenopus fraseri.* This species was described by Boulenger in 1905. As far as distribution is concerned, this species overlaps with *Xenopus tropicalis.* Parker (1936) differentiates *Xenopus tropicalis* and *X. fraseri* by the difference in the size of their eyes, *Xenopus fraseri* having by far the larger eyes. Noble (1924), on the other hand, who had a lot of material available for his investigations, stated that the strong variations in *X. tropicalis* specimens made a definite differentiation from *X. fraseri* seem doubtful. He then voiced the view that *Xenopus fraseri* was not a separate species at all but identical to *Xenopus tropicalis.* Such amendments are not unusual in systematics. In the first overwhelming enthusiasm, some scientists have mistaken long-known animals for new discoveries and described them as such. Where *Xenopus fraseri* is concerned, however, the verdict has not been confirmed yet. Sokol (1960), for

Bufo superciliaris. Bufonidae. Photo: H. Hansen, Aquarium Berlin.

American toad, *Bufo terrestris americanus.* Bufonidae. Above, in axillary amplexus; below, albino. Photos: J. K. Langhammer.

instance, still recognizes *Xenopus fraseri*, whereas Herter (1955) and Rose (1950) no longer list *X. fraseri* as a separate species.

In *Xenopus laevis* and *Xenopus gilli*, to continue with our diagnosis of the species, the horny element of the metatarsal tubercles is absent and, as already said, they have no, or only very small, eye tentacles. *Xenopus laevis* undoubtedly is the most widely distributed *Xenopus*, considering it occurs in all African savannah areas south of the Sahara. In South Africa it is found together with *Xenopus gilli*, but *Xenopus gilli* only covers a modest area of distribution around Cape Town. *Xenopus laevis* is also the largest species and is distinguished from *X. gilli* by its teeth and by the different color of its belly. The belly of *Xenopus laevis* is of a uniform yellowish-white color, while that of *X. gilli* has black specks and patches in addition which partly merge into each other. *Xenopus gilli* was only discovered in 1927, by Rose.

The Platanna, as *Xenopus laevis* is called in South Africa, was described in 1803 by Daudin, though at first it was called *Bufo laevis*. The natives collect *Xenopus laevis*, dry it, and sell it as a health food. *Xenopus clivii* occurs in Ethiopia and in some areas of Kenya; it possesses a black horny element on the metatarsal tubercle and is thus easy to distinguish from *Xenopus laevis*.

Identifying *Hymenochirus*

The differentiation of the species belonging to the genus *Xenopus* is extremely difficult, but the representatives of the genus *Hymenochirus* do not make it any easier for us. Unfortunately, they are even more difficult to identify. Let us therefore begin by listing the characteristics of the genus, those which apply to all species. Here, too, I shall confine myself to the characteristics of importance to the vivarist, the external, obvious ones. They include: rough skin, three claws on the inner toes, webbing between the toes *and* the fingers as well, and a small body size. The average head-trunk length is 30 mm. As opposed to *Xenopus*, the nostrils are on the tip of the snout. All these characteristics apply to *Pseudhymenochirus merlini* as well, the only species of this genus, which was discovered in

Although *Hymenochirus* is the most commonly available pipid, few dealers or aquarists realize they are not simply young *Xenopus*. Besides being much smaller than any *Xenopus*, *Hymenochirus* is greatly flattened, has strong ridges on the head, lacks distinct fleshy tabs and, most importantly, has strongly webbed fingers. *Xenopus* has fingers without visible webs. The taxonomy of *Hymenochirus* is so confused that it is almost impossible to identify adults of this genus. For that reason we will call all the photographs by the oldest name, *Hymenochirus boettgeri.* Photo by Dr. Herbert R. Axelrod.

1920; the only way in which it differs from *Hymenochirus* is the fact that it possesses eye-lids.

How uncertain even the herpetologists are when it comes to determining the *Hymenochirus* species can be seen from the contradictory opinions on the question as to whether the five *Hymenochirus* representatives are, in fact, species or just races. Yes, even the separate classification of the genus *Pseudhymenochirus* is disputed again and again and an incorporation of *Pseudhymenochirus merlini* into the genus *Hymenochirus* has

South American bullfrog, *Leptodactylus pentadactylus.*
Leptodactylidae. Photo: van den Nieuwenhuizen.

Asian spadefoot, *Megophrys nasuta. Pelobatidae.* Photo: J. K.
Langhammer.

Poison arrow frog. Dendrobatidae. Photo: W. Mudrack.

been demanded. In view of the uncertainty of the zoologists, the vivarist can, therefore, do nothing but be content with general characteristics. One consolation after this confession: the larvae—in as far as they have been described—display specific characteristics. This will be dealt with in greater detail under the description of tadpoles.

All *Hymenochirus* species and subspecies known to date come from West Africa. They are *Hymenochirus curtipes, Hymenochirus boulengeri, Hymenochirus boettgeri boettgeri, Hymenochirus boettgeri feae*, and *Hymenochirus boettgeri camerunensis*.

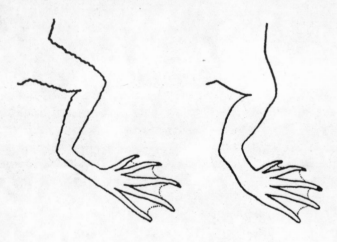

In theory, *Hymenochirus boettgeri* (left) has a much longer tibia and more granular, warty skin than *H. curtipes* and *H. boulengeri* (right). These distinctions are very hard to apply to living aquarium material, however.

According to the latest research and the most recent reports in the literature, a division of the genus *Hymenochirus* into two groups of species ought to be correct: a *Boettgeri* group and the *Curtipes* group. To the *Curtipes* group should also belong, apart from *Hymenochirus curtipes, Hymenochirus boulengeri*. As opposed to the representatives of the *Boettgeri* group, these two share two characteristics: a shorter tibia and a more finely granular skin. But who has the necessary material for comparison available to be able to detect such purely relative distinctions?

In their distribution, too, the two species *H. curtipes* and *H. boulengeri* are neighbors. *Hymenochirus curtipes* occurs in the Lower Congo basin, and *H. boulengeri* inhabits the Central Congo basin. Noble's opinion that *Hymenochirus curtipes* is only found in treeless areas—as opposed to *H. boettgeri* forms which occur in forest areas—has not been confirmed.

The representatives of the *Boettgeri* group are relatively easy to distinguish. The belly of *Hymenochirus boettgeri camerunensis* is covered with numerous speckles and spots. *Hymenochirus boettgeri camerunensis,* as the name indicates, comes from the Cameroons where in 1957 it was collected by the herpetologists Perret and Mertens and described as a new subspecies. *Hymenochirus b. boettgeri,* identified by the notably large "warts" on the flanks and, as already said, the long tibia, is brownish-gray on the top-side and yellow-brown on the belly. *H. b. boettgeri* is the oldest known *Hymenochirus* species. It was described in 1896 as *Xenopus boettgeri. Hymenochirus boettgeri feae,* .an almost black subspecies, can be recognized by the absence of the enlarged "warts" and by the webbing which reaches the tips of both fingers and toes. *Hymenochirus* species (usually just *H. boettgeri* but sometimes *H. curtipes* as well) regularly appear on the market and are offered under fanciful or false names such as "Dwarf Xenopus" or as "African water frogs."

Keeping *Hymenochirus*

As far as keeping is concerned, however, all *Hymenochirus* species make the same modest demands. At temperatures of between 20 and 28° C they are quite content, and since they are hunting most of the time, they are interesting objects of observation.

Atelopid, *Atelopus cruciger*. Atelopidae. Photo: J. K. Langhammer.

Hyla smithi, treefrog. Hylidae. Photo: F. J. Dodd, Jr.

Marsupial frog, *Gastrotheca marsupiata*. Hylidae. Photo: Dr. Otto Klee.

5
Problems with the frog menu?

Xenopus

Instead of giving you a list of all the foods the pipidean frogs like, it is much easier and quicker to tell you what they don't like. They reject very little and eat almost anything, at least frogs of the genus *Xenopus*. Since these species are also the easiest ones to obtain, many vivarists who have decided to keep pipidean frogs will start off with *Xenopus*. If we, then, want to find out the favorite foods of our pets, we offer them a variety

Xenopus is an easy frog to feed because it is not too choosy about its diet. Almost any aquatic insect is eaten, as are most flying types. Mosquito larvae should be excellent, as they are usually easy to obtain and store well. Always keep the aquarium covered, however, so that the adult mosquitoes will not be able to leave the tank. *Xenopus* will eat adult mosquitoes also. Photo by Knaack.

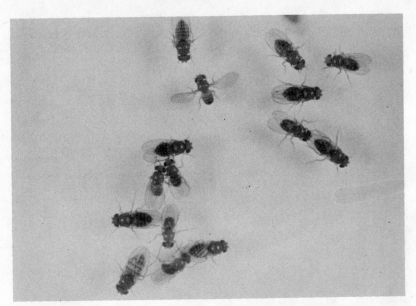

Fruitflies (*Drosophila melanogaster*) are small flies which can be easily and cheaply raised in a small space and are thus excellent as frog food. If the short-winged type is bred, they can be dumped from the culture jars directly into the aquarium. Photo by Imgrund.

of foods and by what they select find out what is acceptable and what is not. This method is tedious. It is easier to study the literature and look for advice there and then to apply the experiences of the experienced. For *Xenopus* we find quite a lot of all sorts of different tips, for pipas unfortunately not so many.

A great help are the stomach examinations carried out by many scientists when they dissect specimens they have found. Analyses of this kind exist of *Xenopus mülleri* and *Xenopus tropicalis,* both of them species which are particularly clever at catching insects flying just above the water surface or dropping on the water. Noble, who carried out the investigations, found numerous termites, ants, beetles, beetle larvae, and tadpoles— of the same species as well as those of more distant relatives—in the stomachs of the species mentioned. From this we conclude that what *Xenopus* eats in nature should be acceptable in confinement as well. For best success offer the frogs tadpoles,

Spring peeper, *Hyla crucifer.* Hylidae. Photo: W. Mudrack.

Eastern chorus frog, *Pseudacris triseriata.* Hylidae. Photo: W. Mudrack.

Pine barrens treefrog, *Hyla andersoni*. Hylidae. Photo: J. K. Langhammer.

Green treefrog, *Hyla caerulea*. Hylidae. Photo: G. Marcuse.

smooth caterpillars, flies, and occasionally even grasshoppers, provided, of course, the time of year permits the gathering of such food. In times of scarcity mealworms can also serve as *Xenopus* food, but the frogs are not all that enthusiastic about this particular diet. Finally, all kinds of food known to the fish culturist are excellently suited as well: *Tubifex,* midge larvae, and *Daphnia.*

For the glutton *Xenopus,* however, these are nothing but miniature portions. A better match for their appetite would be a medium-size earthworm or a piece of liver or meat of the same size. But if you want to offer them a very special delicacy you should occasionally sacrifice a few guppies or give the gourmets a bit of cream cheese from time to time. By the way, breeding guppies as a store of food for frogs undoubtedly has great advantages, provided, of course, there is room for another aquarium.

Tubifex worms have become famous as a food for tropical fishes, and they should not be ignored as frog food. Portions of tubifex worms are available cheaply at most pet shops, and the slight expense is easily made up for when one watches a *Hymenochirus* wrestling with a lively worm. Freeze-dried tubifex are also commonly available. Photo by Dr. Herbert R. Axelrod.

Big frogs need big meals, and *Xenopus* is a big frog. Earthworms, whether the large night crawlers used as bait or the smaller garden types, are enjoyed by all African pipids, although most are too large for *Hymenochirus*. To a greedy-eyed *Xenopus*, however, the largest night crawler is just another tidbit to be forked down as quickly as possible in order to make way for the next piece of food that might come his way. Photo by P. Imgrund.

Hymenochirus

Hymenochirus species are also not choosey in their food requirements, but they specialize on small, slow-moving prey. Their favorite diet consists of *Cyclops, Daphnia,* and *Tubifex,* which can occasionally be supplemented by a feast of midge or mosquito larvae. Their demands can thus be satisfied, without difficulties and without a great deal of expenditure, by supplies from the nearest pet shop.

Australasian green treefrog, *Hyla infrafrenata*. Hylidae. Photo: Dr. Otto Klee.

Hyla gratiosa, bell frog. Hylidae. Photo: W. Mudrack.

For some unknown reason, perhaps related to the flattened head shape, *Pipa* rejects food fishes with high backs, like this *Leuciscus*. A round fish might simply be easier to swallow. Photo by G. J. M. Timmerman.

Pipa

My experiences with pipas are limited to *Pipa pipa,* which is also the species most frequently appearing on the market. It is something of a problem-child where nutrition is concerned. *Pipa* takes nothing but live food as a rule, and although Rabb successfully fed his animals on pieces of liver and meat moved on a bit of wire, the pipas in the Institute of Zoology at Vienna University only accept *Phoxinus phoxinus* (minnows) and other fish which resemble minnows in shape. Fish with a high back, such as *Leuciscus* or *Scardinus,* on the other hand, are hardly attacked at all; with their vertical swimming position, they do not fit into the narrow pipa mouth anyway.

Over and above all the favorite foods cited here, the vivarist is, of course, at liberty to experiment with other types of food as well. No pipid keeper will find these experiments dull.

Small crustaceans such as *Daphnia* are enjoyed by *Hymenochirus* and even by *Xenopus*. The food value of *Daphnia* is much smaller than that of brine shrimp, however. Photo by K. Lerch.

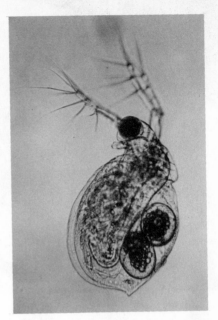

Pipa seems to prefer larger animal food, such as fishes. Europeans find that fishes with the round body shape of *Phoxinus* (below) are readily taken. Photo by G. Senfft.

African treefrog, *Hyperolius fusciventris*. Rhacophoridae. Photo: W. Mudrack.

Arum frog, *Hyperolius horstockii*. Rhacophoridae. Photo: W. Mudrack.

Leopard frog, *Rana pipiens*. Ranidae. Photo: F. J. Dodd, Jr.

Rana pustulosa, pustulose frog. Ranidae. Photo: F. J. Dodd, Jr.

6

Characteristic feeding behavior of pipids

All the rules drawn up by the Baron von Knigge concerning behavior at meal time are broken by the pipids. They use their hands, are greedy and quarrelsome, eat noisily, snap, and even spit. There is one characteristic they all have in common: they are always hungry.

As far as their manners are concerned, one must make allowances. Quite apart from the fact that it was not frogs that Knigge was lecturing to, the pipids always hold their wild feasts under water any way. And if you still feel their manners are inexcusable, I can only suggest you have a go yourself at dining under water. You would soon realize that, with its more or less specialized anatomical and behavioral equipment, a terrestrial animal can do nothing, or hardly anything, under water. Water is, after all, a dense medium, and if a hungry land frog should succeed in catching a fish swimming past under water it would most probably push its tempting prey away again with the water current caused by the snapping of its jaws. Then how is it possible for fully aquatic frogs to get at their prey? How do these species avoid the risk of forever pushing away their own food? Well, Mother Nature has solved this problem, too, for some species in a simple way, but for the pipids in a highly complex way.

Form and shape have been adapted to their function. "The broader the jaws, the larger the mouth" is the rule here, and this leads to a logical conclusion: the larger the mouth, the more water will find room in it when the animal snatches its prey.

Suction becomes correspondingly strong, the victim is sucked in deeply and can no longer escape. This system is found, for instance, in the species *Calyptocephalella gayi.*

At the other end of the scale, as opposed to this primitive solution, there is the "hyoid pump" of the pipids, first described by Willem (1936). Here, a tremendous suction is produced when the frog opens its mouth and, as Sokol (1960) was able to prove, this is due to the curious structure of the ventral parts of the shoulder girdle and girdle musculature. Basically, a two phase complex can be observed in the feeding behavior of pipidean frogs, but only in the *Pipa* species is this basic pattern preserved unchanged. In these frogs the two phases are clearly marked and easy to distinguish:

Phase 1: Hunting stroke and opening the mouth.

Phase 2: The manual work.

Pipa

But let us proceed step by step; the *Pipa* species are proper night-birds, to avoid coining the new term "night-frogs", and they are passive predators. They spend most of their time lying inertly on the bottom of the aquarium and their cold predatory nature does not become apparent until a prey dares to come too close. As quick as a flash they then dart forward, thrust the mouth wide open, and the victim simply disappears between their jaws. Just as quickly, with the help of a backstroke, they return to their place. They are perfect hunting strokes—the inquisitve food fish hardly ever manages to get away. The reach of the hunting strokes depends on the size of the animals. A fully grown *Pipa pipa,* for instance, achieves strokes of up to 10 cm.

After the successful hunting stroke the second phase of the typical feeding behavior begins, the manual work already mentioned. With the fingers widely splayed, the *Pipa* species push their hands in front of the mouth and thus form a kind of weir-basket which prevents the prey from escaping. Bottom material such as pebbles, clusters of algae, etc., is frequently sucked up together with the food animal and has to be spit out again before the food is swallowed.

Rana erythraea. Ranidae. Photo: Dr.Otto Klee.

Hymenochirus

This two phase feeding behavior is strictly adhered to; it also explains why only live, or at least moving, food is accepted. The *Hymenochirus* species also are perfect suction feeders, and predominantly go for live food. Just one fundamental difference characterizes their feeding behavior: the second phase is barely developed. *Hymenochirus* species first and foremost go for planktonic organisms. They are quite unable to catch bigger prey, and this excludes the danger of the food easily getting away again. The hands of *Hymenochirus* species are in any case hardly needed to restrain the prey and, because of the webbing, this would, of course, not be successful anyway. Webbed hands are used to assist with the powerful hunting stroke of these small predators.

Much like the pipas, the *Hymenochirus* species also lie in wait for their victims. There is one quality, however, they do not possess: patience. If no food animal has been swimming past for some time, hunger gets the better of them and they begin to hunt actively. Crawling or swimming, they move over the bottom of the aquarium or glide along the glass walls. Hands and legs are employed to the same degree. Every crevice, every depression, and every hiding place is searched for possible food. If the frog has discovered a *Tubifex* worm buried in the sand, it will hunt it in the same way as it would swimming prey—with a quick and usually successful hunting stroke. *Hymenochirus curtipes* in particular shows itself as a master at the hunting of *Tubifex*. *Hymenochirus boettgeri*, on the other hand, exhibits special hunting talents in free water.

To watch *H. curtipes* hunt for *Tubifex* is particularly interesting. When the frog has spotted a worm—which it does by sight alone—it lowers its head cautiously, draws closer and closer to the prey, and suddenly pounces on it. It immediately has the worm between its jaws and, planting its legs firmly and moving backwards, skillfully pulls and drags the victim out of the sand. The food animal is eaten in no time at all and the hunting continues at characteristic *Hymenochirus* speed.

Xenopus

The representatives of the genus *Xenopus*, finally, are the wildest robber knights among the pipids. Forever hungry, they completely lose control if they sense food nearby. Their waywardness and the hectic speed of their movements thus make it particularly difficult for the observer to make out the typical phases of their feeding behavior. The hunting stroke is barely present any longer. The second phase, on the other hand, can be regarded as refined and highly specialized. The manual work of the *Xenopus* species borders on artistic skill. Snatch and stuffing movements, as Kramer appropriately called them, take turns with gesticulating and wiping movements. Again and again the observer gets the impression that these gluttons are full of panic and fear, thinking the food might be taken away from them.

As a rule, the food is caught by swimming toward it at the utmost speed. Here the frogs of the genus *Xenopus* surpass their pipidean colleagues not only in their activity but also in their quick and determined detection of the prey. The size of the food animal is only of minor importance in this respect. If the animal is small, it disappears instantly; if it is bulkier, the hands are used to push it in and the hind legs to pluck it into shape at the same time or, if necessary, to tear it into pieces. Snatching and stuffing are standard movements in this procedure, applied as much when hunting for *Daphnia* as when devouring a huge earthworm. Even when the prey is able to escape, the disappointed hunter will stuff imaginary pieces of food into his mouth: a typical "vacuum" reaction. When gulping down a large piece of food, the gluttons often draw in their eyes, sometimes one, sometimes both—a very comical looking peculiarity.

Clawed frogs which have been kept for some time become relatively tame. Feeding out of the hand can already be carried out quite easily after a short period. Thus Grimm (1952) reports that after just two weeks his clawed frogs came to the water surface when the glass cover was taken off—especially if they had been fasting for a long period. The more replete *Xenopus* feels, the more it desires rest; a clawed frog who is full is tempted neither by a tasty earthworm nor by a delicious tadpole. But when is a *Xenopus* ever full?

7

Pipids do not believe in the stork

Rain

The pipid keeper who treats his animals well and on top of that develops a little skill may become a pipid breeder over night. That is the simplest but also the most mysterious way. Vivarists, however, have a thirst for knowledge and are, therefore, curious. They are just as deeply interested in the "how" as they are genuinely pleased about the unexpected success. Spawning according to plan and the study of reproductive behavior will, therefore, become their great goal—a goal which many pipid enthusiasts have been waiting to reach for a long time and many will never reach. For pipids do not believe in the stork (they merely fear it as their enemy), but in the rain.

Observations of *Xenopus* species in nature have shown that some of the animals live in very small bodies of water. These miniature lakes dry up regularly, and by this time the inhabitants have disappeared. They have not, of course, dissolved, but have buried themselves deep in the muddy ground which is now covered with a hard crust. There they wait for the rain to release them. When it comes—and in their African homeland the rainy period lasts an entire season—the little *Xenopus* folk will come back to life again. Within just a short period they will make the inguinal embrace in the newly risen waters and eventually shed their spawn.

Artificial inducement

This "reviver", the rain, seems to be missed by the animals in captivity. The good care the animals receive most probably makes them lazy, too. What then shall we do? The vivarist who is forever trying to make conditions as true to nature as possible

The main advantage of carrying eggs and tadpoles on the parent's back is obvious: no drying pools destroy the tadpoles. Any frog that lays its eggs in temporary rain pools faces the possibility of the death of all its tadpoles before any develop legs and can survive on land. *Pipa* does not face this hazard. Photo by H. Pfletschinger.

when furnishing his aquaria and terraria now above all needs to imitate the rain. The drought prior to the rainy season is simulated simply by reducing the water level or, even more simply, by letting the water evaporate. After some time one then replaces the lost water by adding cooler water, and allows the temperature to rise to 28° C. This temperature should be kept constant, if possible. The artificial rainy season undoubtedly stimulates mating; even if the first attempt is unsuccessful, the chances that breeding will yet succeed are great, perhaps not with *Pipa* but definitely with *Hymenochirus* and *Xenopus*.

Naturally, the "rain-making activity" cannot be attempted just at any time. In our region it is best carried out in spring or when there are signs that the animals are already in heat. It is equally important that the animals be given plenty of food during this time.

Many breeders have achieved good success by additional cold storage of the pipids in winter. During the winter months they let the water temperature drop to 18 - 20° C (even lower for *Xenopus*) and do not raise it again until spring. But since during the cool period the temperament of the animals also cools off considerably, the vivarist will get less pleasure out of this method.

Another hint for breeders-to-be: on no account must the breeding aquaria be stocked with too many frogs. Five to eight animals constitute the maximum. If this number is exceeded, the over-population will inhibit the mating impulse of the frogs. If we can clearly distinguish the sexes, the very best solution would be to put a breeding pair into a separate container.

The pipid keeper should definitely attempt to breed his frogs in captivity, for the reproductive behavior in particular is really sensational. Not only that, but the tadpole stage of the pipids also is full of surprises and interesting details. And if all attempts remain absolutely unsuccessful, let me mention what is the last chance so to speak: the use of gonadotrophic agents. Such doses of hormones have to be injected into both sexes, preferably several specimens at once. The most suitable time for this treatment is the early hours of the evening. Usually, the effect of the injections can be observed after just a few hours: the males call, embrace, and in many cases the reproductive products are discharged in a very short time.

Pipa reproduction

If you have read any early natural history encyclopedias published in the 19th century, you will no doubt remember the gruesomely beautiful picture of the "Alveolar Toad". With numerous eggs on its back, sitting on the edge of a pond—that is how the illustrator portrayed it; *Pipa americana* (the former name for *Pipa pipa*) it was called. Despite all inaccuracy, the drawings still show what is so exciting about the life of pipas: the care of the brood.

"Eggs on the back—nothing new whatsoever!" the anuran experts will say. This kind of brood-care is known from other tailless amphibians as well—for instance the American tree

Looking carefully, one can see the skin pouch on the last third of the back of this *Gastrotheca*. Although this frog carries the eggs, normal tadpoles develop, drop off into the axils of plants, and develop in the water there. Photo by G. Marcuse.

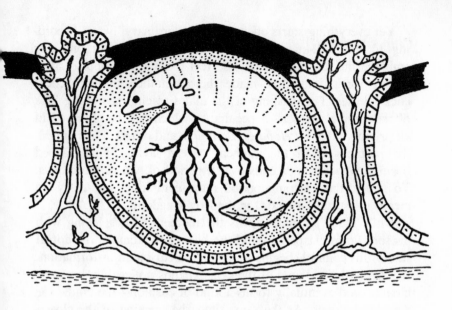

During the development of the *Pipa* egg, the embryo is safely stored in a pouch of skin, but the mother does not actually have any food connection with the embryo. Although the pouch is often called a placenta, it is not really the same as the placenta of mammals, where the embryo depends on the mother for nourishment.

frog *Hyla goeldii,* which carries its eggs about in a skin fold, or the South American pouch frogs, *Gastrotheca,* which transport their brood in a "rucksack" consisting of several skin folds and thus protect them excellently. Such know-alls are partly right, but only partly. For, in its way, the brood-care of pipids is unrivalled, and there is in fact an enormous difference between back transport and back transport. And although the knowledge of pipidean brood-care dates back to the last century, the first detailed descriptions of these species' biology of reproduction were only supplied during the last decade.

The breeding of *Pipa pipa* (the other *Pipa* species are but rarely available on the market) is a real sensation for every vivarist. Not that breeding so seldom succeeds or is so difficult—a little patience and a bit of skill are, however, essential—but a multitude of exciting details turns the observation of mating into an adventure.

Yet everything starts off in such an "ordinary" way. According to the well-known frog habit, the *Pipa* males one day embrace the females, which also feel the mating impulse, after having for a long time made their metallic-sounding "click-click" noises. The clasping of the males reaches round the hips of the female partner—a peculiarity which can be observed in all primitive frogs, *Pelobates, Bombina*, and others. Thus united, the partners await the moment of egg laying. This clasped position sometimes extends over a period of two or more days. To many, this clasping period may seem long, but it by no means constitutes a record in the frog kingdom.

While the *Pipa* male awaits the moment of egg laying with his fore limbs clasped around the hips of the female, the dorsal skin of his comrade begins to undergo a curious transformation. A sharply defined area of the skin expands noticeably, becomes bloated, and eventually forms a kind of cushion—the cradle for the pipa toadlets. At the same time, the opening of the cloaca also becomes enlarged. It goes without saying that during this period, too, the animals rise to the water surface for fresh air, but now, of course, they do it together.

Some time before egg laying begins, a growing restlessness can be observed, particularly in the female. More than once we notice movements of the female which give the impression that the embraced animal was trying to escape from the grip of the male. But suddenly the time has come: the *Pipa* couple rises from the bottom—at first one believes they are going for air again—and move up towards the water surface. Just below the water surface the two frogs rotate around their longitudinal axis and, with a perfect somersault, they begin their return journey to the bottom of the aquarium. This performance is repeated several times without any eggs being laid. Spawning begins only after a great many of these "turnovers" as Mr. and Mrs. Rabb call these somersaults of the pipids. Before spawning the observant spectator will notice a marked retraction and protrusion of the funnel-like cloacal opening of the female which, finally, is firmly pressed against the abdomen of the male.

During one of the following rotations the first eggs appear, and from now on further eggs are shed during nearly every "turnover". The eggs are discharged at the culmination point

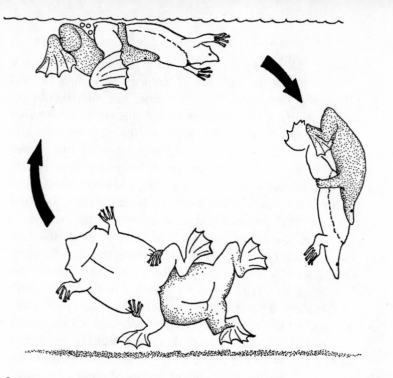

Summary of the spawning behavior of *Pipa*. Notice the "turnover" or somersault before and after the laying of eggs at the surface. After Rabb and Rabb.

(the vertex), so to speak, of the rotation, when the frogs remain motionless for about a second in a horizontal position, belly upwards. Fertilization takes place at the same time. The eggs first drop onto the belly side of the male, and slowly roll along between the frogs toward the area of the bloated dorsal region of the female. Every time there are about three to six eggs which thus, not least because of the active support of the male who aids and guides the forward gliding of the eggs with his shaking movements, reach the "baby cradle". After every phase the animals return to the bottom of the aquarium and, motionless, remain there in a curious position: head down, they rest on the bottom at an acute angle of about 30 degrees. These breaks last for 5 or 10 minutes, then the pair comes up for air again, and a little later rises for another egg producing somersault.

Spawning takes several hours. Rabb's animals once took three hours, and in the Institute of Zoology at Vienna University the process took much the same time. The number of eggs laid varies greatly and, according to the literature, between 40 and 114 eggs can be expected. Some of the eggs laid are lost immediately—partly they drop to the ground owing to the over violent movements of the male, partly they are brushed off during the following somersaults. Last but not least, the number of eggs also depends on the size of the female's back, as often more eggs are laid than can find room in the soft dorsal skin.

Shortly after spawning, half an hour later at most, the two animals separate. By characteristically pressing the back forward and simultaneously stretching the front and hind limbs, the female informs its partner that the mission is over. The male then immediately separates from its mate, supplies itself with fresh air, and soon gives out its longing "click-click" again.

The spawning method just described—during a belly-uppermost position of the frog couple—is unrivalled within the salientian world; among the different genera of pipids, however, it is, with small variations, found everywhere.

Spawning *Hymenochirus*

In *Hymenochirus*, males in mating condition call constantly and frequently try to embrace passing females. The excitement slowly grows, and soon the characteristic "dancing" of the males in heat can be observed. Rabb and Rabb (1963) have described this form of behavior in detail: scraping, hasty movements with the feet, and the arms gesticulating as if in the inguinal embrace. The dance is usually followed by further monotonous calling. Once the male in heat has discovered an animal of the same species, it advances sideways, toward the flank, and as soon as the desired object moves it skillfully tries to clasp it. But often these attempts remain nothing but attempts. For, if the animal in heat has come across a second male, the sexually wrongly assessed comrade of the same species "growls" and quickly the suitor lets go of him. Females also, when they are already spent or simply not willing, are very clever at getting out of the clasp again: They stiffly stretch back their

A pair of *Hymenochirus* ready for spawning. As a rule, the male (left) is smaller than the egg-filled female (right). Some males also have a creamy spot or area on the side behind the front leg. Photo by B. Haas.

hind legs, and, if necessary, emphasize their displeasure by additional shaking of the body.

The males rejected in this way soon begin to call again. While doing so they slightly raise the anterior end of the body above the ground, and it often looks as if they were standing on their finger-tips. At the same time, this position is a sort of threat, a warning for other males in heat: I am here, dare not come too close! When the mating impulse is not present these reactions die down. The two authors Osterdahl and Olsson (1963) tried to distinguish between an attacking position and a calling position but, in my opinion, these two kinds of behavior cannot be differentiated. If a calling frog failed to adopt the characteristic position, it could not be recognized as the producer of the sound.

In most frogs the male holds the spawning female behind the front legs. In pipids and other primitive frogs, however, the females are clasped in front of the hind legs, a process called inguinal amplexus. Photos by B. Haas.

The mating calls of the *Hymenochirus* males can be compared to the ticking of an alarm clock. Apart from this one, there is, however, another sound—the rejecting growling sound already mentioned. The females which are ready to spawn are recognized by their willingness. Rivals, on the other hand, are noted mainly by their acoustic signals. Over and above that, there will undoubtedly be impulses which can be perceived through the vibration reception of the lateral organs and the well developed sense of smell; these are the vibrations produced simultaneously with the growling sound, and the secretions of the axillary gland.

If the mating movements of a male are answered with an "inviting" forward movement of the female, clasping will immediately take place. In the typical pipidean way, the male encloses the inguinal region of its partner with the front legs

The spawning cycle of *Hymenochirus* is very similar to that of *Pipa*, involving somersaults and the laying of eggs at the surface. After Osterdahl and Olsson.

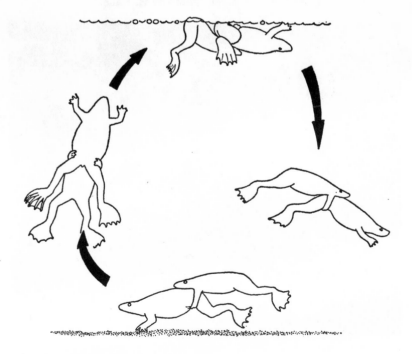

and presses itself closely against the back of the female. Pumping movements—loosening and renewed pressing of the arms—also are frequently observed in clasping males. Finally, the male gives its partner an occasional "wipe" across the head with its clawed hind legs— another phenomenon which occurs in all pipids and is thought to be a gesture of stimulation. In *Hymenochirus* it precedes spawning anyway. The female then, only a few minutes after clasping has begun, bends its back and, taking the initiative, rises to the water surface with the male. There the couple rotate in the "belly uppermost position." Both animals raise the vents of their cloaca above the water surface and discharge their reproductive products. By simultaneously describing rowing movements, to and fro, with the hind legs, the frog couple usually manages to remain in this position for one or two seconds.

The eggs of *Hymenochirus* are laid in small groups. Each egg is separate and not connected to its neighbor by gelatinous string as is common in many other frogs. Eggs which sink or adhere to plants seldom hatch. Photo by B. Haas.

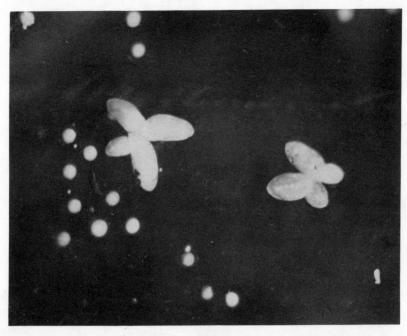

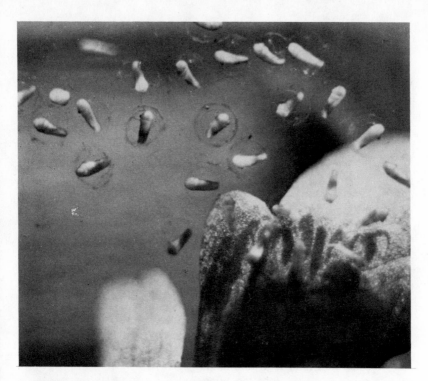

Fertile *Hymenochirus* eggs which have remained at the surface develop rapidly, the first tadpoles appearing in less than two days. The jelly-like egg capsules are plainly visible around these late embryos. Photo by B. Haas.

Not every rotation in the dorsal position ends in spawning. The cycle of movements is repeated several times, but only the second or a later rotation successfully results in the discharge of spawn. Afterwards the couple swims back to the bottom of the aquarium where they remain for a longer period, one to five minutes. Then the spawning process starts all over again. During every spawning excursion just a few eggs are deposited on the water surface; as a rule they remain attached to the thin surface film, but a few may be caused to sink by the later activities of the frogs. The number of spawning processes varies greatly. According to the literature, the spawning rotations observed were anything between 50 (Osterdahl and Olsson 1963) and 346 (Rabb and Rabb 1963), with, in the highest case, more

Developmental stages of *Hyme-nochirus.* Photos by B. Haas.

Fully formed tadpole before eruption of legs.

Well-formed hind legs and small fore leg buds.

Mature tadpole before absorption of the tail.

Froglets of *Hymenochirus* are relatively large when compared with their inch-long mother. In a few weeks the body will enlarge and the head will take on the more pointed shape characteristic of the genus. Photo by B. Haas.

than 1000 eggs being shed. The duration of egg laying also varied between one and seven hours.

Rabb and Rabb (1963) have discovered and described a further peculiarity where *Hymenochirus* is concerned and that is the shedding of spawn by the female in the absence of clasping or previous clasping. I have never observed this phenomenon.

Xenopus reproduction

A pattern of behavior similar to that described with regard to *Pipa* and *Hymenochirus* species can also be seen in the mating and egg laying of *Xenopus*. In their *Hymenochirus* work, Rabb and Rabb mention *Xenopus laevis* as well and their breeding successes with this species. According to the data supplied by them, *Xenopus laevis*, too, exhibits all the characteristic behavior noted in *Hymenochirus*, with the sole exception of the "dance". Although Rabb's data consist of only a table, they can be regarded as being the "most detailed" found in the literature. A contradiction? No. This somewhat strange problem has a quite different reason: *Xenopus* has been bred often, and usually with an economic motive. Breeding turned out to be easy, and yet hardly any scientific records are available.

The Hogben test

About 50 years ago *Xenopus* was nothing but a strange, rare animal to scientists, and to vivarists almost a fabulous creature, provided they had heard about the platanna*, as *Xenopus* is called in its country of origin, at all. It was not until the 1920's that *Xenopus laevis*—the species known longest—was kept by European vivarists. And then came the year 1930, so vital for the entire genus. In this year the scientist Hogben published his work on a method of the early diagnosis of pregnancy, and the principal character in this new test was *Xenopus laevis*. Until then only a few zoologists and perhaps a small group of enthusiastic naturalists had been interested in the clawed frogs. But now, all at once, medical laboratories all over the world required *Xenopus*. The Hogben test, as this method was named by Crew 9 years later, attracted attention everywhere. The demand for platannas rose enormously.

Yet the Hogben test was not the first relatively reliable method of early diagnosis of actual conception. In 1927 the Austrian medical scientists Aschheim and Zonder had been able to prove that, shortly after conception, the urine of pregnant women can cause the same effects as do the hormones of the anterior lobe of the hypophysis (or pituitary gland). Based on this experience, they developed a method of early diagnosis which they tried out with infant mice. This method is particularly reliable. A drawback, however, proved to be the long duration of the test, which always took four days. Hogben's method, on the other hand, supplied equally reliable results after just a few hours.

* *Platanna* from the word "Plathander" = flat hands.

But how is the Hogben test carried out? The method is simple: the urine of the woman to be examined is injected subcutaneously into the dorsal lymph sac of the *Xenopus* female. That is all there is to it. If the reaction is positive, the female frog will spawn after five to eight or at most within 12 hours, with quantities of up to 2000 eggs no exception. If no spawn is discharged after up to a maximum of 18 hours, the test result is negative, and the woman is not pregnant.

The Hogben test is as simple as that, and it is hardly surprising to hear that mass introductions of *Xenopus laevis* reached the research laboratories. After the first successes of the Hogben test, several thousand specimens were supplied to England alone, and Elkan (1938) feared in all seriousness that the extinction of the clawed frogs was not far away. Not much later, World War II put an unexpected stop to the booming frog export. All further supplies for the European laboratories ceased and all at once the continuation of the Hogben test was dependent solely on the successful artificial cultivation of clawed frogs. But breeding would not succeed. With regret, Birkenbach stated in 1941 that a successful cultivation could not be expected in Germany, despite the active support of zoologists. But immediately afterward the breeding problem of *Xenopus* was solved after all. Gasche (1943) and his assistants developed a method whereby the successful cultivation no longer depended on chance and had become a simple matter.

What was this discovery? Nothing but the treatment of the male as well as the female *Xenopus* with the gonadotrophic factors of pregnancy urine, the so-called "Prolan". In those days Prolan was available in powder form, and thus the medication was no problem either. The successes were tremendous: up to 1000 eggs per couple, repeatable a month later. Mass production could begin. But Gasche supplied some further advice of which one hint in particular is of interest to us. He writes: "The containers (with the treated breeding couples) are covered with a cloth so that the animals are not disturbed." And they were not disturbed; they were neither disturbed nor watched when they laid their eggs. This is the problem mentioned at the beginning of the chapter, that despite easy breeding, information on individual modes of behavior is scarce. Something else that suddenly became the center of interest for the scientists was the tadpole of *Xenopus*. For in it they saw the ideal animal for developmental physiology and embryology studies and experiments.

Spawning

As far as the reproductive behavior of *Xenopus* species is known, it shall now be described. Basically it resembles that of the other pipidean genera. The males in heat embrace the females in the inguinal region after having indicated their desire to mate with a loud "crike-crike". A certain "nervousness" is not rare either in males feeling the mating impulse. When the male has found a female partner the pumping and wiping behavior already described with regard to *Pipa* and *Hymenochirus* can be observed. The pumping movements in particular are distinct, and at the same time we hear a new cadence, described by Grimm (1952) as the "clasping sound": "tuck-tuck".

Another interesting phenomenon is a rotating movement of the couple which is undoubtedly instigated by the male and of which different authors have given various interpretations. With a jerk, the animals rotate around their longitudinal axis, and the female becomes akinetic (rigid, stiff) during this process. Its arms are stretched forward, diagonally, and its legs are stretched back stiffly.

The duration of clasping varies and can be anything between a few hours and two days. Grimm (1952b) has observed even longer periods. The clasped females begin to spawn spontaneously. During rotating movements, which are sometimes very similar to the "turnovers" of *Pipa* and *Hymenochirus* but not so regular or marked, the eggs are usually shed singly and fertilized by the male. The eggs stick to plants and stones and sometimes to the tube of the aerator. Bushnell (1957) cites that egg clusters of three to four eggs each are laid, but I did not find this statement confirmed. If there is any disturbance, egg laying usually comes to an abrupt halt. During reproduction the animals react very sensitively to outside stimuli.

As a rule, spawning takes place during the night. The breeder does not usually discover the "surprise" until the following morning. A hint to the disappointed: usually the frogs continue

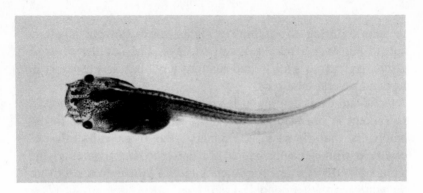

Early tadpole of *Xenopus laevis*. Although the tentacles or "antennae" are not visible, their bases are conspicuous. In life the tadpole hangs head-downward. Photo by G. J. M. Timmerman.

Dorsal and ventral views of the mature *Xenopus* tadpole. The tentacles are still conspicuous. Photo by G. J. M. Timmerman.

to spawn during the following nights, as egg laying is often spread out over a period of several days. The number of eggs discharged varies greatly and may be anything between just a few and several hundreds.

Good success is continuously reported with regard to *Xenopus* pairs kept in open ponds. The other side of the coin, unfortunately, is that in such "containers" the frogs can only be observed with difficulty or not at all. According to a report by Kahmann (1949), a few forgotten *Xenopus* larvae even survived the winter in such a pond.

It is advisable to separate parent animals and spawn immediately after spawning, as the frogs regard the eggs as a welcome delicacy. Incidentally, the spawn of native frogs can occasionally be used as *Xenopus* food. The aquarium with the eggs must be well aerated until the larvae hatch and then again until the tadpoles begin to swim independently. Only then—when the tadpoles have become "fledged"—does the work of the vivarist begin. Reproduction is taken care of by Nature and is ruled by instinct and impulse; but the thriving of the brood depends on the diligence and, not least, the skill of the breeder. A few hints given in the next chapters may be a small but useful help to the vivarist in this respect.

Just a few words about the skin

Sometimes, especially after mating, the behavior of pipidean frogs become quite wild, and one gets the impression that they were madly trying to get out of their skin. This is in fact just what they are doing. There is, however, no direct connection between the shedding of the skin and the reproductive behavior, but the great excitement during the inguinal embrace and spawning undoubtedly stimulates and helps to speed up the changing of the skin.

Shedding of the skin, the periodic peeling-off of the epidermis, is an ancient characteristic of all anurans including, of course, the pipids. This changing of the skin runs parallel with the casting-off of the claws, as long as the individual species possess claws. Occasionally—some authors say regularly—the skin-shreds which have been slipped off are swallowed.

8

The curious tadpoles of the genus *Hymenochirus*

"They can be recognized by their tadpoles!" This could be the guiding principle for all vivarists who have difficulty in differentiating the two *Hymenochirus* species, *H. curtipes* and *H. boettgeri* (these two are the only species regularly available on the market). To confuse the two tadpoles is impossible, as they look so different, and their behavior differs so much. And yet, in many resepcts they are similar, and in many aspects they clearly show themselves as pipidean larvae.

H. curtipes

But it is the egg we should begin with, not the tadpole. The eggs of *Hymenochirus curtipes,* including the very sticky external gelatinous covering, have a diameter of roughly 2 mm and float on the water surface or adhere to the plants. The color is brownish; the number of eggs deposited varies, but on an average about 150 eggs are laid each time, Many eggs perish, of course. Almost none of the eggs which have sunk to the bottom of the aquarium—when the mature animals come up for air they are often pushed off the water surface—will develop, and the eggs adhering to the water plants also are more at risk than those which have remained on the water surface. Adequate aeration is particularly important for successful breeding.

The larvae hatch after one and a half to two days. The water temperature is of considerable importance, since if it is below 22° C it is fairly certain that the first breeding attempt will fail. During the first six days—six on an average—of their larval life the hatched tadpoles hang suspended from plants or the glass walls of the tank, wriggling, attached by their adhesive gland (not paired). They are of a brown color and the size of their body is a mere 4 mm. But as soon as the tadpoles have left this hanging stage of their lives behind and start to swim independently in search of food, their predatory nature becomes apparent. Slowly and cautiously they glide along just below the water surface, horizontally, and one needs to be very observant to notice the ceaseless vibrating of the transparent tip of the tail. These small fellows take in air as well, although minute external gills are present—relics rather than respiratory instruments, by the look of them.

And what do the larvae of *Hymenochirus curtipes* feed on? *Cyclops* above all, and the vivarist is advised to offer plenty of this "powder-food". For, the hunting success of these small robber knights is relatively slight; furthermore, many of the animals caught turn out to be too large (e.g. *Daphnia*) and are spat out again. If a food animal comes near the tadpole, the predator darts toward the victim and tries to suck it up through its mouth tube. The term "mouth tube" is by no means a fanciful expression or even an exaggeration: the larvae of *Hymenochirus curtipes* indeed possess a curiously shaped mouth. It consists of a tube directed upwards. When the mouth is opened, the mouth tube bends forward, diagonally, and the suction produced with the aid of the hyobranchial apparatus results in the food being sucked into the oral cavity. Then the mouth closes again, and the animal caught is no longer able to escape. The water, finally, is discharged through small openings which are present in pairs, the spiracles. Horny jaws or labial teeth which occur in most tadpoles are absent in *Hymenochirus*, and they also lack a filtration system or a "weir apparatus".

The larval life of *Hymenochirus curtipes* lasts for an average of 60 to 70 days, then metamorphosis takes place. After just 30 days the hind legs can be identified; the fore limbs, however, do not appear until just before metamorphosis is completed. The newly metamorphosed young frogs average one centimeter in length. To feed these juniors is no problem. At this stage they already take *Tubifex, Daphnia*, and the larvae of *Corethra,* and, by and large, almost any food is welcome—provided there is plenty of it.

As simple as this metamorphosis of the tadpoles into proper frogs (that is, miniature editions at first) may appear, as naturally as the development continues step by step, so significant is this period in the life of anurans. In the life of a frog metamorphosis is undoubtedly *the* climax, the great turning-point above all in the way of life, since as a rule the aquatic life is exchanged for a terrestrial life. That this can only come about with extensive changes is understandable—the transformations extend far beyond the loss of the tail and the degeneration of the gills. The alimentary canal, for instance, is adapted to the new conditions when the (in the majority of cases) vegetarian tadpoles turn into carnivorous toads and frogs. With the pipids we have not been introduced to a standard model but to primitive forms of the frog family tree, but for their larvae, too, metamorphosis still remains the vital stage of development.

The tadpole of *Hymenochirus curtipes* displays the dorsal mouth typical of the genus. The unpigmented tail tip is not readily apparent. Top, ventral view, bottom, dorsal view.

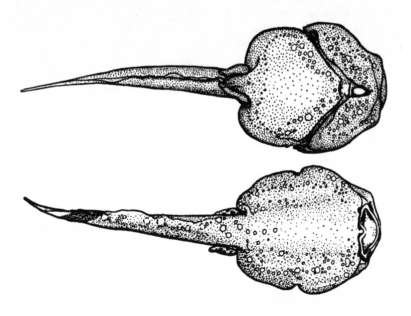

H. boettgeri

As compared to *H. curtipes* spawn, the eggs of *Hymenochirus boettgeri* are a little smaller (1.2 to 1.5 mm, including the gelatinous covering) and perhaps a shade lighter in color. The number of eggs deposited is the same as that of *H. curtipes*. After about one day the $2\frac{1}{2}$ mm long larvae hatch, only to spend their first four to six days hanging like commas everywhere in the breeding tank. They, too, have an adhesive gland and attach themselves with the aid of its secretions.

Once the larvae have made the brave plunge into free water, the characteristics which distinguish them from *H. curtipes* can be clearly recognized—especially the shape of the body and the color. *Hymenochirus boettgeri* is slimmer and, to stick to the frog kingdom with our comparisons, bears a greater resemblance to the standard tadpole shape as we know it in such forms as *Rana*. The eyes are strikingly large. The larvae are dark-gray, the ventral side is notably lighter. Over and above that, there is a marked silver sheen of the body and the absence of a colorless, i.e., pigmentless, tip of the tail as we describe it with regard to

The tadpoles of *Hymenochirus curtipes* (top) and *H. boettgeri* (bottom) are easier to distinguish than the adults. Notice especially the stubby tail with an unpigmented tip in *H. curtipes*.

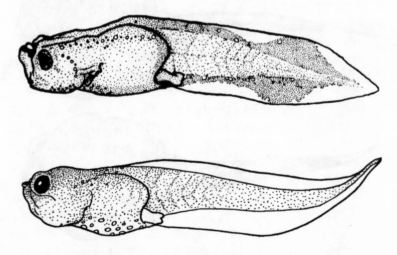

H. curtipes. The pigment arrangement on the tail appears to be the most obvious characteristic of *H. curtipes* tadpoles, and its absence a sure characteristic of the species *H. boettgeri.* The diagram clearly shows the difference.

The vivarist who has seen both forms of larvae can easily differentiate *H. boettgeri* and *H. curtipes,* and even the description of their peculiarities given here should be sufficient to make reliable diagnoses possible. For all those who feel uncertain I shall mention a further differential characteristic: The larvae of *Hymenochirus boettgeri* are far more active than those of *H. curtipes.* Like fish fry, they move through the water (the tip of the tail serves as a driving engine) and seek to satisfy their chronic hunger.

Cyclops are excellently suited as food animals, but to these more skilfull hunters we can already offer *Daphnia* and even pieces of *Tubifex* as well. As with the *H. curtipes* larvae, the food is caught by suction and snapping. With the aid of their hyobranchial apparatus, they produce a powerful suction which draws the victims into the mouth tube. The position of the mouth tube—as in *H. curtipes* directed upwards when closed and when open diagonally bent forward—makes me suggest a hypothesis which is backed up by the preference for remaining below the water level: in nature the *Hymenochirus* tadpoles "graze" on the water surface. Because the supra-aquatic fauna of tropical waters is particularly rich, quite apart from the insects dropping onto the water surface, it constitutes an ideal "pasture" for the *Hymenochirus* larvae.

Just how important this nekton (= minute swimming organisms on the surface "membrane" of the water) is as a source of food can be seen from an investigation carried out by two Argentinian biologists (Rapoport and Sanchez 1963). For five minutes these two scientists fished, or better, skimmed, at the surface of a river, and in this short period caught more than 600 organisms. The bulk of these consisted of collembolans (spring-tails, wingless insects). In stagnant waters, lakes, ponds, and pools the number is usually much higher still. For the *Hymenochirus* tadpoles this would be a proper "land of milk and honey", and it is by no means improbable that scientific evidence of this will soon be submitted. Ambitious vivarists are, of course, also very welcome to carry out observations or experiments on the subject.

That tadpoles graze on the water surface is nothing new at all. Herpetologists know of the most varied types among the anuran larvae: there are those whose mouth region is transformed into a sucking disc with the aid of which they can attach themselves to stones even in very fast running water, and others whose flat and slender body has been pre-shaped for an existence in small tree hollows filled with water. These adaptations are not confined to systematic groups, and appear in the greatest variety of families, yes, even within large genera. This is also the case with the experts of the "water surface grazers" which have become known mainly from the family Microhylidae but can be found among the pelobatids, dendrobatids, and hylids (tree frogs) as well.

Back to *Hymenochirus*! About one month after the onset of active feeding or the free swimming stage, the metamorphosis approaches its end. The foot stumps appear on approximately the 12th, the arms on the 20th day, provided the tadpoles have been well looked after and adequately fed until then. The biggest specimens measure about 2 cm, and as a rule they are slightly larger than the *H. curtipes* tadpoles. The duration of metamorphosis is of course influenced by the water temperature as well. Rabb's tadpoles, which were kept at 20-24° C, needed as long as six weeks to become metamorphosed. The tadpoles continue to feed throughout metamorphosis although the displacement and transformation of the mouth—from a tube directed upwards into a typical frog mouth—falls into this period.

All in all, the carnivorous (flesh eating) tadpoles of the two *Hymenochirus* species are extremely interesting pets, in many aspects perhaps more interesting than some fish broods, and to rear them is not difficult either. Perhaps further *Hymenochirus* species will yet appear on the animal market, possibly with tadpoles which display yet other kinds of behavior. For many empty pages still exist in the large breeding book of this genus; and because of them there are no barriers to discourage the inquiring mind of vivarists. They still have many possibilities to win fame.

9
Tadpoles with antennae

Xenopus tadpoles

These "antennae", I must admit, have given me special food for thought, because the tadpoles of *Xenopus* I mean to describe here possess so many peculiarities that it is difficult to decide which character to describe. The antennae, or . . .? Well, I have stuck to the antennae for they at least can be clearly recognized at first sight: two long filaments beginning at the sides of the mouth slit and reaching far forward. Apart from the tentacles, as the "antennae" should be called more correctly, one is immediately struck by the curious position and movement in the water of the *Xenopus* juniors. The head is forever lowered sideways and through rhythmic beating of the tip of the tail they glide through their element in this posture. The head segment is more or less transparent and only the relatively large eyes can be recognized as dark spots. The mouth opens and closes ceaselessly—various observers counted about 40 to 50 times per minute—, and with this we have come to one of the most interesting structures of the *Xenopus* tadpoles: their filtration and "weir" apparatus.

Mouth movements

If you interpret these pumping movements of the mouth as pure respiratory (breathing) activity, you are only partly right. First and foremost, water is pumped through here and at the same time food is filtered. Briefly, the structure of the filtration apparatus is as follows: the gill arches of *Xenopus* larva carry a net-like, highly vascular filter consisting of tiny folds. This filter is situated in front of the gill slits and is able to catch even the smallest particles. Through negative pressure in the oral cavity the water is sucked in when the mouth opens. The tadpole then closes its mouth and the water inside it is squeezed through the gill filter and leaves the body through the paired spiracles. The trapped food particles are mixed with mucus— a sticky substance secreted by numerous small glands—, shaped into tiny balls and, via a ciliated canal, despatched into the pharynx. A valve system regulates the water flow in this process.

The long tentacles or *"antennae"* of Xenopus tadpoles are very characteristic of *Xenopus.* The body shape is more normal than that of *Hymenochirus* tadpoles. Photo by G. J. M. Timmerman.

Apart from this function of the filtration apparatus in the supply of nourishment, it also has a secondary function as a respiratory organ. Schober (1949) proved this with a very simple experiment. One *Xenopus* tadpole was put into water with a high oxygen content and another into boiled water (= low oxygen content). Then the number of times the tadpoles came up to the water surface for air were counted. It turned out that the larva in low oxygen water came up 4 - 5 times as often as the larva in high oxygen water. This proves that the tadpoles utilize the oxygen in the water for respiration. First and foremost, however, the *Xenopus* larvae breathe through the lungs, and every four to six minutes one can see them quickly swimming to the surface with the tentacles drawn back to get fresh air.

Feeding
The description of the complicated filtration apparatus of the *Xenopus* tadpoles may have impressed some of you, but

breeders-to-be will ask in horror, "What shall we feed?" Don't worry—the nutrition of the *Xenopus* babies is not really complicated at all. But the composition of the menu is somewhat unusual. More important than the "what" is the "how", and by this I mean the consistency of the food. Only the very finest food particles can be fed or ingested by the larvae. Larger morsels getting inside the filtration apparatus in most cases—especially in regard to younger larvae—lead to the death of the animal. It is of utmost importance, therefore, to use particularly "finely granular" food which should be mixed with the water to form a suspension. In brief: mashed food for the babies of *Xenopus*.

As a standard food tested by numerous breeders and applied with the best of success, we today use stinging-nettle tea. This can be purchased quite cheaply under the name "Herba urtica". Gasche (1943) recommended that some clover flour should be added to it which, in his opinion, is more suitable than crushed thread algae used in the past. Other recommended additives include dried *Daphnia* and yarrow powder. The meals are prepared as follows: stinging-nettle tea (with or without additives) is stirred into a thin pulp with a little water and this is poured through a small linen bag into the tank. The residues are best squeezed again by wringing the linen bag. So much for the normal diet. In addition the occasional infusoria menu is recommended, easily grown if you put lettuce leaves or hay into a preserving jar filled with water. Finally I can readily recommend the occasional addition of a piece of yolk from a hard-boiled egg. Schneider (1956) described still more delicacies and for the sake of completeness I shall record his recipes, too. 5 g of oat flour are mixed well with 25 mg of dried yeast (finely cellular, if possible) and a little water, and this pulp is poured into 100 cm^3 of boiling water. Until cooling this needs to be stirred from time to time so that no skin forms. Dosage: 1 - 2 teaspoons per 100 tadpoles daily.

In many cases this type of food makes the water turn cloudy, and some vivarists will be horrified when they "see green" in their aquaria. Don't worry! The tadpoles are tireless filterers and will soon make the water become clear again. Within just a few hours the coloration or turbidity of the water should have disappeared again; but if the tank is still not clean after about 8 hours, this is a sign that the breeder has mixed too much food—calculated according to the number of tadpoles—into the water. In fact, the correct amount of food should be determined as soon as possible since residues very quickly foul the water, and left-overs become covered with fungi. Regular suction cleaning of the bottom with an ordinary pipette and an occasional water change will certainly do no harm.

Growth

The free-swimming larval life of the *Xenopus* offspring lasts for an average of 5 to 8 weeks. Development depends very much on the water temperature and particularly on correct feeding. Where there is an over population, disturbances of growth or irregular developmental progress are constantly observed. For a tank of 20 x 20 cm for instance, Dickinson recommends a maximum of 100 tadpoles, but if possible still fewer larvae should be reared in an aquarium of this size. The free swimming stage of the tadpoles is preceded by a period of two to three days during which the larvae hang suspended, and more or less motionless, from the walls of the aquarium and the water plants. They hatch about two days after the eggs have been deposited. Bushnell's tadpoles hatched on the 3rd day at the earliest.

If offered favorable conditions, *Xenopus* tadpoles grow very quickly. At a water temperature of roughly 24 - 26° C and with the best of feeding, they reach the stately size of 5 to 6 cm within 30 or 40 days, and by then the onset of metamorphosis is no longer far away. Metamorphosis takes 10 days. When it is over the small frogs have "closed down" their filtration apparatus and do as other frogs do—as far as food is concerned and their greed. *Tubifex,* midge larvae, *Daphnia*—everything is gratefully accepted.

It takes the frogs about one year to reach their full size. They become sexually mature after the same length of time, the males earlier than the females. According to Dickinson, it takes 2 years from egg to maturity but this statement is opposed by contradictory information of various other authors.